PRESIDENTIAL CHRONICLES

PRESIDENTIAL CHRONICLES

JOEL HAWKSLEY

J & Washington Network

CONTENTS

Presidential Chronicles: Poetic Homage to Leadership

The following poems individually stand as tributes, not critiques, to each presidential term, aiming to honor the leaders who shouldered the immense responsibility of the presidency. Recognizing the challenge of setting aside biases in political philosophy, I hope these verses can be approached with reverence for the individuals who undertook what many consider the most demanding job in the world.

I acknowledged that differing political perspectives exist, and I invite readers to appreciate the intention of paying homage rather than finding fault in the work. While critics may emerge, I sincerely hope that any critiques are offered with a certain level of thoughtful consideration.

The poems can be intricately woven together, linked by a repeating stanza that emphasizes the overarching theme:

"From freedom's spark to modern grace,
Through trials met and victory's pace,
Each tale inscribed in history's rhyme,
Presidential hands that shaped our time."

The final stanza serves as a conclusive culmination, summarizing the collective journey from 1789 to 2024:

> "In forty-six poems, the journey's complete,
> Presidents in sequence, a historical feat.
> From Washington's dawn to Biden's stride,
> In freedom's embrace, the nation's guide."

The intent is to provide a comprehensive and unified tribute to all the presidents, acknowledging their roles in shaping the nation's history. When this is done, the poem is Titled *"In Freedom's Embrace: A Presidential Journey."*

George Washington

From fields of war, a leader born,
Founding Father, a nation sworn.
Through strife and hope, the union won,
George Washington, a rising sun.

In history's pages, his deeds align,
A name forever, in freedom's sign.
The first to guide with steady hand,
George Washington, our chosen stand.

CHAPTER 2

John Adams

In independence' early light,
John Adams stood, a patriot's might.
Through challenges and foreign haze,
He served his term with steady gaze.

A voice for law, in freedom's name,
John Adams upheld the nation's flame.
In history's scroll, his name does glisten,
A leader true, by duty smitten.

Thomas Jefferson

From quill to parchment, words profound,
Thomas Jefferson's ideas unbound.
Declaration penned with fervent might,
In liberty's glow, he took his flight.

A vision vast, of westward sprawl,
A polymath, in knowledge tall.
A third president, in times aplomb,
Thomas Jefferson, the nation's psalm.

James Madison

In halls of debate, Madison stood,
A Constitution shaped in brotherhood.
Through Federalist pens and states' accord,
He guided the ship, the union moored.

Father of Bill, the amendments' rhyme,
James Madison's legacy, enduring time.
In governance dance, a measured stride,
A president true, with laws as guide.

CHAPTER 5

James Monroe

Era of good feelings, a soothing balm,
James Monroe's presidency, a calming calm.
Monroe Doctrine, in foreign lands,
A leader's touch, in peace expands.

From Virginian roots, to the presidential throne,
James Monroe's reign, a harmony known.
In history's gaze, his name to linger,
A presidential voice, a statesman's finger.

CHAPTER 6

John Quincy Adams

Son of a father, in statesmanship bred,
John Quincy Adams, where intellect led.
Through diplomatic paths and servant's heart,
He played his part, a leader's art.

From foreign realms to the House's chair,
A president's legacy, just and fair.
In history's annals, a chapter inscribed,
John Quincy Adams, in wisdom described.

CHAPTER 7

Andrew Jackson

A frontier son with fiery might,
Andrew Jackson, in battles' sight.
From Hermitage to the presidency's door,
Old Hickory's reign, a tempest's roar.

In triumphs hailed and trails of tears,
A leader bold, sparking fears.
Through duels and deeds, a nation's lore,
Andrew Jackson, forevermore.

CHAPTER 8

Martin Van Buren

From Kinderhook, a president arose,
Martin Van Buren, through ebbs and flows.
In economic tides and political sea,
He navigated with skill and glee.

A vice to Jackson, a successor true,
Van Buren's term, a steward's view.
In history's tapestry, woven fine,
Martin Van Buren's legacy, benign.

CHAPTER 9

William Harrison

A brief tenure, a leader's fate,

William Henry Harrison, brief and great.

In thirty days, a presidency gone,

Yet, remembered still, at dawn's first dawn.

A hero of Tippecanoe, a general's might,

In history's brevity, a fleeting light.

A leader gone with the wind's soft kiss,

William Henry Harrison, in memory's bliss.

CHAPTER 10

John Tyler

In Harrison's wake, Tyler sworn,
A president's role, new burdens borne.
From annexation talks to statesman's strife,
Tyler navigated the presidential life.

A Whig by name, but Democrat's kin,
In history's script, his chapters spin.
John Tyler's term, a shifting sand,
A leader's legacy, shaped by the land.

CHAPTER 11

James K. Polk

Manifest destiny, a vision clear,
James K. Polk, a pioneer.
From Oregon trails to Mexican strife,
He shaped a nation's expanding life.

Through treaties penned and battles won,
In history's echo, Polk's name is spun.
A leader's task, a manifest quest,
James K. Polk, in the Westward zest.

CHAPTER 12

Zachary Taylor

A general's heart, a soldier's grace,
Zachary Taylor took his place.
From battles fought to the presidency's chair,
A leader true, with a soldier's flair.

In fields of conflict, and political stage,
Taylor's legacy, a measured page.
A brief tenure, a leader's fate,
Zachary Taylor, at freedom's gate.

CHAPTER 13

Millard Fillmore

In Taylor's wake, Fillmore stood,
A president true, as best he could.
From compromise to foreign shore,
Fillmore's term, a leader's lore.

In tumultuous times, a steady hand,
A leader's role, by duty manned.
Millard Fillmore, in history's scroll,
A presidency marked, a nation's goal.

CHAPTER 14

Franklin Pierce

A northern man, a southern strife,
Franklin Pierce, in presidential life.
Through compromise and sectional fray,
He led the nation, come what may.

From Gadsden Purchase to bleeding land,
A leader's choices shaped the sand.
In history's chapters, a nuanced tale,
Franklin Pierce, in times frail.

CHAPTER 15

James Buchanan

In tumultuous times, Buchanan's stand,
A nation divided, in his hand.
Through secession threats and states' divide,
Buchanan navigated with faltering stride.

A president's burden, a nation's fate,
James Buchanan, at history's gate.
In retrospect, a tumultuous span,
A leader's role, in a troubled plan.

CHAPTER 16

Abraham Lincoln

A towering figure, in top hat and strife,
Abraham Lincoln, the savior of life.
Through civil war and Emancipation's ink,
He led the nation, on freedom's brink.

From Gettysburg's fields to a fateful night,
A leader true, in history's light.
Abraham Lincoln, a martyr's grace,
A name forever in freedom's embrace.

CHAPTER 17

Andrew Johnson

In Lincoln's shadow, a Southern son,
Andrew Johnson, the task begun.
Through reconstruction's challenges deep,
A leader guided by principles to keep.

From impeachment threat to rights bestowed,
Johnson's term in history flowed.
A president's role in a nation's dance,
Andrew Johnson, in time's expanse.

CHAPTER 18

Ulysses S. Grant

From Union's general to the presidential post,
Ulysses S. Grant, a leader engrossed.
Through Reconstruction's trial and strife,
He sought to bind the nation's life.

In battles fought and policies set,
A presidency with both triumph and debt.
Grant's legacy, a complex weave,
A leader steadfast, in history to cleave.

CHAPTER 19

Rutherford B. Hayes

In disputed times, Hayes took command,
A presidency shaped by a delicate hand.
Through Compromise's choice and electoral haze,
He led the nation in post-war days.

A leader in a time of transition,
Rutherford B. Hayes, a measured mission.
In history's record, a balanced view,
A president's role, firm and true.

CHAPTER 20

James A. Garfield

From educator to leader's fate,
James A. Garfield, a name ornate.
Through Civil War and Congress's hall,
A president's rise, a nation's call.

In tragic end, a life cut short,
Garfield's legacy, in history's court.
A leader lost to a fateful day,
James A. Garfield, in memory's sway.

CHAPTER 21

Chester A. Arthur

In Garfield's wake, Arthur sworn,
A presidency in reform born.
From spoils to civil service line,
Arthur's term, a reformed design.

A leader's role, a balance found,
Chester A. Arthur, on duty bound.
In history's pages, a name indelible,
A president's term, sometimes incredible.

CHAPTER 22

Grover Cleveland (1st)

From Buffalo to Washington's chair,
Grover Cleveland, a leader rare.
In non-consecutive terms, a unique feat,
A president's role, a steady beat.

Through economic trials and labor's cry,
Cleveland's term, a watchful eye.
In history's mirror, a dual gaze,
A leader true, in different days.

CHAPTER 23

Benjamin Harrison

In Harrison's time, a frontier's kin,
A president's term, a nation's spin.
From Civil War memories to economic might,
Harrison's leadership, in history's light.

A leader's hand in tariffs' sway,
Benjamin Harrison, in presidential array.
In cycles of time, his name etched,
A leader's term, in history fetched.

Grover Cleveland (2nd)

Back again in the presidential hall,
Grover Cleveland, answering the call.
From tariff woes to labor's strife,
A leader's role, a nation's life.

In non-consecutive terms, a unique story,
Cleveland's return, a political glory.
A president's hand in varied days,
Grover Cleveland, in history's gaze.

CHAPTER 25

William McKinley

In Ohio's embrace, McKinley rose,
A leader's path, where destiny flows.
Through war and markets, his tenure's might,
McKinley led, in history's light.

In Spanish-American conflict's fire,
A president's role, a nation's desire.
William McKinley, in freedom's name,
A legacy carved in the political game.

CHAPTER 26

Theodore Roosevelt

A Rough Rider's spirit, a conservation quest,
Theodore Roosevelt, a president blessed.
From trust-busting days to Panama's canal,
A leader dynamic, standing tall.

In the arena of reform and foreign might,
Roosevelt's legacy, a daring flight.
A president's voice in progressive lore,
Theodore Roosevelt, forevermore.

CHAPTER 27

William Howard Taft

From Roosevelt's shadow, Taft emerged,
A presidency's mantle, firmly surged.
In trust's embrace and Dollar Diplomacy's call,
Taft led the nation, in progress enthralled.

A justice served and a gavel's weight,
Taft's term, in history's gate.
A leader's task in times untamed,
William Howard Taft, a presidency named.

CHAPTER 28

Woodrow Wilson

In World War's shadow, Wilson stood,
A leader's role, misunderstood.
Through League debates and peace's plea,
Wilson shaped a new diplomacy.

In Fourteen Points and Treaty's fight,
A president's vision, in history's light.
Woodrow Wilson, in freedom's name,
A legacy marked, in the world's acclaim.

CHAPTER 29

Warren G. Harding

In roaring twenties' carefree swing,
Warren Harding, a leader's wing.
From scandals faced to arms race's tone,
Harding's term, in history's zone.

A presidency brief, a life's reprieve,
Harding's legacy, in shadows weave.
A leader's path, in fortune and fall,
Warren G. Harding, remembered in call.

CHAPTER 30

Calvin Coolidge

Silent Cal, with few words spoken,
Calvin Coolidge's leadership unbroken.
In laissez-faire days and prosperity's hum,
A leader's calm, a nation's strum.

From Boston roots to presidential chair,
Coolidge's term, a steadfast air.
A leader quiet, with a nation's trust,
Calvin Coolidge, in history's thrust.

Herbert Hoover

From commerce chambers to Oval's chair,
Herbert Hoover faced a nation's stare.
Through market's crash and Depression's grip,
Hoover's term, a leadership trip.

In public works and Hoover Dam's rise,
A president's efforts to mend the ties.
A leader burdened, in history's view,
Herbert Hoover, in times askew.

CHAPTER 32

Franklin D. Roosevelt

Amidst the Great Depression's woe,
Franklin Roosevelt, a leader's glow.
In fireside chats and New Deal's grace,
He guided the nation to a hopeful space.

Through World War's storm and freedom's quest,
FDR's legacy, a president's best.
A leader's heart in trying years,
Franklin Roosevelt, through joys and tears.

CHAPTER 33

Harry S. Truman

From Potsdam's talks to a troubled start,
Harry Truman played his part.
In atomic days and Cold War's chill,
Truman led, with iron will.

A Fair Deal sought and UN's embrace,
A president's term in history's trace.
Harry S. Truman, in freedom's call,
A leader's stand, through rise and fall.

Dwight D. Eisenhower

From war's command to peace's reign,
Dwight Eisenhower, a leader's gain.
Through highways' weave and Sputnik's flight,
Eisenhower led, in Cold War's light.

A military mind in politics' sway,
Eisenhower's legacy, in history's display.
A leader's path in strategic might,
Dwight D. Eisenhower, a steady sight.

CHAPTER 35

John F. Kennedy

In Camelot's aura and Cuban strife,
John F. Kennedy, a charismatic life.
Through moonlit dreams and civil rights stand,
He led the nation with a youthful hand.

A New Frontier and a tragic end,
Kennedy's legacy, a nation's friend.
A leader's vision, in history's rhyme,
John F. Kennedy, an enduring time.

CHAPTER 36

Lyndon B. Johnson

In Kennedy's wake, Johnson took command,
A presidency marked by Vietnam's sand.
Through civil rights laws and War on Poverty,
Johnson led with a complex legacy.

A leader's heart in tumultuous days,
Lyndon B. Johnson, in history's maze.
In the Oval's chair, a burden worn,
A president's role, through roses and thorn.

CHAPTER 37

Richard Nixon

From Checkers' speech to Watergate's storm,
Richard Nixon faced a troubled norm.
In foreign realms and détente's embrace,
Nixon's term, a complex grace.

A leader's fall in scandal's bind,
Nixon's legacy, a troubled mind.
A presidency marked by strife,
Richard Nixon, in political life.

Gerald Ford

In Nixon's wake, Ford ascends,
A presidency born of troubled trends.
Through pardon's choice and inflation's bane,
Ford led, a brief refrain.

A leader's task in turbulent days,
Gerald Ford, in history's gaze.
A presidency, brief yet strong,
In times when trust was proved wrong.

Jimmy Carter

From Georgia's fields to the Oval's door,
Jimmy Carter, a leader more.
Through Camp David talks and energy strife,
Carter led, in a challenging life.

A presidency marked by hostages' plight,
Carter's legacy, a peacekeeper's light.
A leader's heart, in humble grace,
Jimmy Carter, in history's embrace.

CHAPTER 40

Ronald Reagan

In Hollywood's glow to politics' stage,
Ronald Reagan, a leader's sage.
Through Cold War's end and economic soar,
Reagan led, with conservative lore.

A shining city on a hill's command,
Reagan's legacy, a leader grand.
A presidency marked by hopeful might,
Ronald Reagan, in freedom's light.

CHAPTER 41

George H. W. Bush

From CIA chief to the presidential seat,
George H. W. Bush, a leader discreet.
Through Desert Storm and Soviet's fall,
Bush led the nation, answering the call.

A presidency marked by steady hand,
Bush's legacy, in history's land.
A leader's path in Gulf War's claim,
George H. W. Bush, a patriot's aim.

CHAPTER 42

Bill Clinton

In saxophone's tune and tech's embrace,
Bill Clinton, a leader's grace.
Through budget battles and NAFTA's sway,
Clinton led, in a booming day.

A presidency marked by scandal's fire,
Clinton's legacy, a complex lyre.
A leader's charm, a nation's song,
Bill Clinton, in history's throng.

George W. Bush

From Texas ranch to the Oval's might,
George W. Bush, a leader's fight.
Through 9/11's shock and Iraq's quest,
Bush led, in a turbulent test.

A presidency marked by war's demand,
Bush's legacy, in freedom's hand.
A leader's path, in divided land,
George W. Bush, in history's strand.

CHAPTER 44

Barack Obama

From Chicago streets to the White House glow,
Barack Obama, a leader's show.
Through healthcare debates and Bin Laden's end,
Obama led, with a message to send.

A presidency marked by hope's refrain,
Obama's legacy, in history's gain.
A leader's vision in change's dance,
Barack Obama, in freedom's advance.

CHAPTER 45

Donald Trump

From business towers to the political storm,
Donald Trump, a leader's norm.
Through tweets and tariffs, a presidency bold,
Trump led, in a story yet untold.

A presidency marked by polarized view,
Trump's legacy, in history's hue.
A leader's impact, in a nation's clash,
Donald Trump, in freedom's flash.

Joe Biden

From Delaware's roots to the Oval's chair,
Joe Biden, a leader aware.
Through pandemic trials and climate's call,
Biden leads, in a challenging sprawl.

A presidency marked by unity's plea,
Biden's legacy, in history's sea.
A leader's task, a nation's blend,
Joe Biden, as time transcends.

CHAPTER 47

In Freedom's Embrace: A Presidential Journey

From fields of war, a leader born,
Founding Father, a nation sworn.
Through strife and hope, the union won,
George Washington, a rising sun.

In history's pages, his deeds align,
A name forever, in freedom's sign.
The first to guide with steady hand,
George Washington, our chosen stand.

From freedom's spark to modern grace,
Through trials met and victory's pace,
Each tale inscribed in history's rhyme,
Presidential hands that shaped our time.

In independence' early light,

John Adams stood, a patriot's might.
Through challenges and foreign haze,
He served his term with steady gaze.

A voice for law, in freedom's name,
John Adams upheld the nation's flame.
In history's scroll, his name does glisten,
A leader true, by duty smitten.

From freedom's spark to modern grace,
Through trials met and victory's pace,
Each tale inscribed in history's rhyme,
Presidential hands that shaped our time.

From quill to parchment, words profound,
Thomas Jefferson's ideas unbound.
Declaration penned with fervent might,
In liberty's glow, he took his flight.

A vision vast, of westward sprawl,
A polymath, in knowledge tall.
A third president, in times aplomb,
Thomas Jefferson, the nation's psalm.

From freedom's spark to modern grace,
Through trials met and victory's pace,
Each tale inscribed in history's rhyme,
Presidential hands that shaped our time.

In halls of debate, Madison stood,
A Constitution shaped in brotherhood.

Through Federalist pens and states' accord,
He guided the ship, the union moored.

Father of Bill, the amendments' rhyme,
James Madison's legacy, enduring time.
In governance dance, a measured stride,
A president true, with laws as guide.

From freedom's spark to modern grace,
Through trials met and victory's pace,
Each tale inscribed in history's rhyme,
Presidential hands that shaped our time.

Era of good feelings, a soothing balm,
James Monroe's presidency, a calming calm.
Monroe Doctrine, in foreign lands,
A leader's touch, in peace expands.

From Virginian roots, to the presidential throne,
James Monroe's reign, a harmony known.
In history's gaze, his name to linger,
A presidential voice, a statesman's finger.

From freedom's spark to modern grace,
Through trials met and victory's pace,
Each tale inscribed in history's rhyme,
Presidential hands that shaped our time.

Son of a father, in statesmanship bred,
John Quincy Adams, where intellect led.

Through diplomatic paths and servant's heart,
He played his part, a leader's art.

From foreign realms to the House's chair,
A president's legacy, just and fair.
In history's annals, a chapter inscribed,
John Quincy Adams, in wisdom described.

From freedom's spark to modern grace,
Through trials met and victory's pace,
Each tale inscribed in history's rhyme,
Presidential hands that shaped our time.

A frontier son with fiery might,
Andrew Jackson, in battles' sight.
From Hermitage to the presidency's door,
Old Hickory's reign, a tempest's roar.

In triumphs hailed and trails of tears,
A leader bold, sparking fears.
Through duels and deeds, a nation's lore,
Andrew Jackson, forevermore.

From freedom's spark to modern grace,
Through trials met and victory's pace,
Each tale inscribed in history's rhyme,
Presidential hands that shaped our time.

From Kinderhook, a president arose,
Martin Van Buren, through ebbs and flows.

In economic tides and political sea,
He navigated with skill and glee.

A vice to Jackson, a successor true,
Van Buren's term, a steward's view.
In history's tapestry, woven fine,
Martin Van Buren's legacy, benign.

From freedom's spark to modern grace,
Through trials met and victory's pace,
Each tale inscribed in history's rhyme,
Presidential hands that shaped our time.

A brief tenure, a leader's fate,
William Henry Harrison, brief and great.
In thirty days, a presidency gone,
Yet, remembered still, at dawn's first dawn.

A hero of Tippecanoe, a general's might,
In history's brevity, a fleeting light.
A leader gone with the wind's soft kiss,
William Henry Harrison, in memory's bliss.

From freedom's spark to modern grace,
Through trials met and victory's pace,
Each tale inscribed in history's rhyme,
Presidential hands that shaped our time.

In Harrison's wake, Tyler sworn,
A president's role, new burdens borne.

From annexation talks to statesman's strife,
Tyler navigated the presidential life.

A Whig by name, but Democrat's kin,
In history's script, his chapters spin.
John Tyler's term, a shifting sand,
A leader's legacy, shaped by the land.

From freedom's spark to modern grace,
Through trials met and victory's pace,
Each tale inscribed in history's rhyme,
Presidential hands that shaped our time.

Manifest destiny, a vision clear,
James K. Polk, a pioneer.
From Oregon trails to Mexican strife,
He shaped a nation's expanding life.

Through treaties penned and battles won,
In history's echo, Polk's name is spun.
A leader's task, a manifest quest,
James K. Polk, in the Westward zest.

From freedom's spark to modern grace,
Through trials met and victory's pace,
Each tale inscribed in history's rhyme,
Presidential hands that shaped our time.

A general's heart, a soldier's grace,
Zachary Taylor took his place.

From battles fought to the presidency's chair,
A leader true, with a soldier's flair.

In fields of conflict, and political stage,
Taylor's legacy, a measured page.
A brief tenure, a leader's fate,
Zachary Taylor, at freedom's gate.

From freedom's spark to modern grace,
Through trials met and victory's pace,
Each tale inscribed in history's rhyme,
Presidential hands that shaped our time.

In Taylor's wake, Fillmore stood,
A president true, as best he could.
From compromise to foreign shore,
Fillmore's term, a leader's lore.

In tumultuous times, a steady hand,
A leader's role, by duty manned.
Millard Fillmore, in history's scroll,
A presidency marked, a nation's goal.

From freedom's spark to modern grace,
Through trials met and victory's pace,
Each tale inscribed in history's rhyme,
Presidential hands that shaped our time.

A northern man, a southern strife,
Franklin Pierce, in presidential life.

Through compromise and sectional fray,
He led the nation, come what may.

From Gadsden Purchase to bleeding land,
A leader's choices shaped the sand.
In history's chapters, a nuanced tale,
Franklin Pierce, in times frail.

From freedom's spark to modern grace,
Through trials met and victory's pace,
Each tale inscribed in history's rhyme,
Presidential hands that shaped our time.

In tumultuous times, Buchanan's stand,
A nation divided, in his hand.
Through secession threats and states' divide,
Buchanan navigated with faltering stride.

A president's burden, a nation's fate,
James Buchanan, at history's gate.
In retrospect, a tumultuous span,
A leader's role, in a troubled plan.

From freedom's spark to modern grace,
Through trials met and victory's pace,
Each tale inscribed in history's rhyme,
Presidential hands that shaped our time.

A towering figure, in top hat and strife,
Abraham Lincoln, the savior of life.

Through civil war and Emancipation's ink,
He led the nation, on freedom's brink.

From Gettysburg's fields to a fateful night,
A leader true, in history's light.
Abraham Lincoln, a martyr's grace,
A name forever in freedom's embrace.

From freedom's spark to modern grace,
Through trials met and victory's pace,
Each tale inscribed in history's rhyme,
Presidential hands that shaped our time.

In Lincoln's shadow, a Southern son,
Andrew Johnson, the task begun.
Through reconstruction's challenges deep,
A leader guided by principles to keep.

From impeachment threat to rights bestowed,
Johnson's term in history flowed.
A president's role in a nation's dance,
Andrew Johnson, in time's expanse.

From freedom's spark to modern grace,
Through trials met and victory's pace,
Each tale inscribed in history's rhyme,
Presidential hands that shaped our time.

From Union's general to the presidential post,
Ulysses S. Grant, a leader engrossed.

Through Reconstruction's trial and strife,
He sought to bind the nation's life.

In battles fought and policies set,
A presidency with both triumph and debt.
Grant's legacy, a complex weave,
A leader steadfast, in history to cleave.

From freedom's spark to modern grace,
Through trials met and victory's pace,
Each tale inscribed in history's rhyme,
Presidential hands that shaped our time.

In disputed times, Hayes took command,
A presidency shaped by a delicate hand.
Through Compromise's choice and electoral haze,
He led the nation in post-war days.

A leader in a time of transition,
Rutherford B. Hayes, a measured mission.
In history's record, a balanced view,
A president's role, firm and true.

From freedom's spark to modern grace,
Through trials met and victory's pace,
Each tale inscribed in history's rhyme,
Presidential hands that shaped our time.

From educator to leader's fate,
James A. Garfield, a name ornate.

Through Civil War and Congress's hall,
A president's rise, a nation's call.

In tragic end, a life cut short,
Garfield's legacy, in history's court.
A leader lost to a fateful day,
James A. Garfield, in memory's sway.

From freedom's spark to modern grace,
Through trials met and victory's pace,
Each tale inscribed in history's rhyme,
Presidential hands that shaped our time.

In Garfield's wake, Arthur sworn,
A presidency in reform born.
From spoils to civil service line,
Arthur's term, a reformed design.

A leader's role, a balance found,
Chester A. Arthur, on duty bound.
In history's pages, a name indelible,
A president's term, sometimes incredible.

From freedom's spark to modern grace,
Through trials met and victory's pace,
Each tale inscribed in history's rhyme,
Presidential hands that shaped our time.

From Buffalo to Washington's chair,
Grover Cleveland, a leader rare.

In non-consecutive terms, a unique feat,
A president's role, a steady beat.

Through economic trials and labor's cry,
Cleveland's term, a watchful eye.
In history's mirror, a dual gaze,
A leader true, in different days.

From freedom's spark to modern grace,
Through trials met and victory's pace,
Each tale inscribed in history's rhyme,
Presidential hands that shaped our time.

In Harrison's time, a frontier's kin,
A president's term, a nation's spin.
From Civil War memories to economic might,
Harrison's leadership, in history's light.

A leader's hand in tariffs' sway,
Benjamin Harrison, in presidential array.
In cycles of time, his name etched,
A leader's term, in history fetched.

From freedom's spark to modern grace,
Through trials met and victory's pace,
Each tale inscribed in history's rhyme,
Presidential hands that shaped our time.

Back again in the presidential hall,
Grover Cleveland, answering the call.

From tariff woes to labor's strife,
A leader's role, a nation's life.

In non-consecutive terms, a unique story,
Cleveland's return, a political glory.
A president's hand in varied days,
Grover Cleveland, in history's gaze.

From freedom's spark to modern grace,
Through trials met and victory's pace,
Each tale inscribed in history's rhyme,
Presidential hands that shaped our time.

In Ohio's embrace, McKinley rose,
A leader's path, where destiny flows.
Through war and markets, his tenure's might,
McKinley led, in history's light.

In Spanish-American conflict's fire,
A president's role, a nation's desire.
William McKinley, in freedom's name,
A legacy carved in the political game.

From freedom's spark to modern grace,
Through trials met and victory's pace,
Each tale inscribed in history's rhyme,
Presidential hands that shaped our time.

A Rough Rider's spirit, a conservation quest,
Theodore Roosevelt, a president blessed.

From trust-busting days to Panama's canal,
A leader dynamic, standing tall.

In the arena of reform and foreign might,
Roosevelt's legacy, a daring flight.
A president's voice in progressive lore,
Theodore Roosevelt, forevermore.

From freedom's spark to modern grace,
Through trials met and victory's pace,
Each tale inscribed in history's rhyme,
Presidential hands that shaped our time.

From Roosevelt's shadow, Taft emerged,
A presidency's mantle, firmly surged.
In trust's embrace and Dollar Diplomacy's call,
Taft led the nation, in progress enthralled.

A justice served and a gavel's weight,
Taft's term, in history's gate.
A leader's task in times untamed,
William Howard Taft, a presidency named.

From freedom's spark to modern grace,
Through trials met and victory's pace,
Each tale inscribed in history's rhyme,
Presidential hands that shaped our time.

In World War's shadow, Wilson stood,
A leader's role, misunderstood.

Through League debates and peace's plea,
Wilson shaped a new diplomacy.

In Fourteen Points and Treaty's fight,
A president's vision, in history's light.
Woodrow Wilson, in freedom's name,
A legacy marked, in the world's acclaim.

From freedom's spark to modern grace,
Through trials met and victory's pace,
Each tale inscribed in history's rhyme,
Presidential hands that shaped our time.

In roaring twenties' carefree swing,
Warren Harding, a leader's wing.
From scandals faced to arms race's tone,
Harding's term, in history's zone.

A presidency brief, a life's reprieve,
Harding's legacy, in shadows weave.
A leader's path, in fortune and fall,
Warren G. Harding, remembered in call.

From freedom's spark to modern grace,
Through trials met and victory's pace,
Each tale inscribed in history's rhyme,
Presidential hands that shaped our time.

Silent Cal, with few words spoken,
Calvin Coolidge's leadership unbroken.

In laissez-faire days and prosperity's hum,
A leader's calm, a nation's strum.

From Boston roots to presidential chair,
Coolidge's term, a steadfast air.
A leader quiet, with a nation's trust,
Calvin Coolidge, in history's thrust.

From freedom's spark to modern grace,
Through trials met and victory's pace,
Each tale inscribed in history's rhyme,
Presidential hands that shaped our time.

From commerce chambers to Oval's chair,
Herbert Hoover faced a nation's stare.
Through market's crash and Depression's grip,
Hoover's term, a leadership trip.

In public works and Hoover Dam's rise,
A president's efforts to mend the ties.
A leader burdened, in history's view,
Herbert Hoover, in times askew.

From freedom's spark to modern grace,
Through trials met and victory's pace,
Each tale inscribed in history's rhyme,
Presidential hands that shaped our time.

Amidst the Great Depression's woe,
Franklin Roosevelt, a leader's glow.

In fireside chats and New Deal's grace,
He guided the nation to a hopeful space.

Through World War's storm and freedom's quest,
FDR's legacy, a president's best.
A leader's heart in trying years,
Franklin Roosevelt, through joys and tears.

From freedom's spark to modern grace,
Through trials met and victory's pace,
Each tale inscribed in history's rhyme,
Presidential hands that shaped our time.

From Potsdam's talks to a troubled start,
Harry Truman played his part.
In atomic days and Cold War's chill,
Truman led, with iron will.

A Fair Deal sought and UN's embrace,
A president's term in history's trace.
Harry S. Truman, in freedom's call,
A leader's stand, through rise and fall.

From freedom's spark to modern grace,
Through trials met and victory's pace,
Each tale inscribed in history's rhyme,
Presidential hands that shaped our time.

From war's command to peace's reign,
Dwight Eisenhower, a leader's gain.

Through highways' weave and Sputnik's flight,
Eisenhower led, in Cold War's light.

A military mind in politics' sway,
Eisenhower's legacy, in history's display.
A leader's path in strategic might,
Dwight D. Eisenhower, a steady sight.

From freedom's spark to modern grace,
Through trials met and victory's pace,
Each tale inscribed in history's rhyme,
Presidential hands that shaped our time.

In Camelot's aura and Cuban strife,
John F. Kennedy, a charismatic life.
Through moonlit dreams and civil rights stand,
He led the nation with a youthful hand.

A New Frontier and a tragic end,
Kennedy's legacy, a nation's friend.
A leader's vision, in history's rhyme,
John F. Kennedy, an enduring time.

From freedom's spark to modern grace,
Through trials met and victory's pace,
Each tale inscribed in history's rhyme,
Presidential hands that shaped our time.

In Kennedy's wake, Johnson took command,
A presidency marked by Vietnam's sand.

Through civil rights laws and War on Poverty,
Johnson led with a complex legacy.

A leader's heart in tumultuous days,
Lyndon B. Johnson, in history's maze.
In the Oval's chair, a burden worn,
A president's role, through roses and thorn.

From freedom's spark to modern grace,
Through trials met and victory's pace,
Each tale inscribed in history's rhyme,
Presidential hands that shaped our time.

From Checkers' speech to Watergate's storm,
Richard Nixon faced a troubled norm.
In foreign realms and détente's embrace,
Nixon's term, a complex grace.

A leader's fall in scandal's bind,
Nixon's legacy, a troubled mind.
A presidency marked by strife,
Richard Nixon, in political life.

From freedom's spark to modern grace,
Through trials met and victory's pace,
Each tale inscribed in history's rhyme,
Presidential hands that shaped our time.

In Nixon's wake, Ford ascends,
A presidency born of troubled trends.

Through pardon's choice and inflation's bane,
Ford led, a brief refrain.

A leader's task in turbulent days,
Gerald Ford, in history's gaze.
A presidency, brief yet strong,
In times when trust was proved wrong.

From freedom's spark to modern grace,
Through trials met and victory's pace,
Each tale inscribed in history's rhyme,
Presidential hands that shaped our time.

From Georgia's fields to the Oval's door,
Jimmy Carter, a leader more.
Through Camp David talks and energy strife,
Carter led, in a challenging life.

A presidency marked by hostages' plight,
Carter's legacy, a peacekeeper's light.
A leader's heart, in humble grace,
Jimmy Carter, in history's embrace.

From freedom's spark to modern grace,
Through trials met and victory's pace,
Each tale inscribed in history's rhyme,
Presidential hands that shaped our time.

In Hollywood's glow to politics' stage,
Ronald Reagan, a leader's sage.

Through Cold War's end and economic soar,
Reagan led, with conservative lore.

A shining city on a hill's command,
Reagan's legacy, a leader grand.
A presidency marked by hopeful might,
Ronald Reagan, in freedom's light.

From freedom's spark to modern grace,
Through trials met and victory's pace,
Each tale inscribed in history's rhyme,
Presidential hands that shaped our time.

From CIA chief to the presidential seat,
George H. W. Bush, a leader discreet.
Through Desert Storm and Soviet's fall,
Bush led the nation, answering the call.

A presidency marked by steady hand,
Bush's legacy, in history's land.
A leader's path in Gulf War's claim,
George H. W. Bush, a patriot's aim.

From freedom's spark to modern grace,
Through trials met and victory's pace,
Each tale inscribed in history's rhyme,
Presidential hands that shaped our time.

In saxophone's tune and tech's embrace,
Bill Clinton, a leader's grace.

Through budget battles and NAFTA's sway,
Clinton led, in a booming day.

A presidency marked by scandal's fire,
Clinton's legacy, a complex lyre.
A leader's charm, a nation's song,
Bill Clinton, in history's throng.

From freedom's spark to modern grace,
Through trials met and victory's pace,
Each tale inscribed in history's rhyme,
Presidential hands that shaped our time.

From Texas ranch to the Oval's might,
George W. Bush, a leader's fight.
Through 9/11's shock and Iraq's quest,
Bush led, in a turbulent test.

A presidency marked by war's demand,
Bush's legacy, in freedom's hand.
A leader's path, in divided land,
George W. Bush, in history's strand.

From freedom's spark to modern grace,
Through trials met and victory's pace,
Each tale inscribed in history's rhyme,
Presidential hands that shaped our time.

From Chicago streets to the White House glow,
Barack Obama, a leader's show.

Through healthcare debates and Bin Laden's end,
Obama led, with a message to send.

A presidency marked by hope's refrain,
Obama's legacy, in history's gain.
A leader's vision in change's dance,
Barack Obama, in freedom's advance.

From freedom's spark to modern grace,
Through trials met and victory's pace,
Each tale inscribed in history's rhyme,
Presidential hands that shaped our time.

From business towers to the political storm,
Donald Trump, a leader's norm.
Through tweets and tariffs, a presidency bold,
Trump led, in a story yet untold.

A presidency marked by polarized view,
Trump's legacy, in history's hue.
A leader's impact, in a nation's clash,
Donald Trump, in freedom's flash.

From freedom's spark to modern grace,
Through trials met and victory's pace,
Each tale inscribed in history's rhyme,
Presidential hands that shaped our time.

From Delaware's roots to the Oval's chair,
Joe Biden, a leader aware.

Through pandemic trials and climate's call,
Biden leads, in a challenging sprawl.

A presidency marked by unity's plea,
Biden's legacy, in history's sea.
A leader's task, a nation's blend,
Joe Biden, as time transcends.

From freedom's spark to modern grace,
Through trials met and victory's pace,
Each tale inscribed in history's rhyme,
Presidential hands that shaped our time.

In forty-six poems, the journey's complete,
Presidents in sequence, a historical feat.
From Washington's dawn to Biden's stride,
In freedom's embrace, the nation's guide.

CHAPTER 48

Presidential Legacy: A Verse of America's Journey

From freedom's spark to modern grace,
Through trials met and victory's pace,
Each tale inscribed in history's rhyme,
Presidential hands that shaped our time.

From freedom's spark to modern grace,
They faced the dawn, each in their place,
Founders' vision, torch alight,
A nation forged, through day and night.

Through trials met and victory's pace,
From wars endured to rights embraced,
Leaders strode, with guiding hand,
United States, across the land.

Each tale inscribed in history's rhyme,
With triumphs etched and trials climb,
From humble roots to soaring might,
Each president, a guiding light.

Presidential hands that shaped our time,
From liberty's bell to modern's chime,
Though paths may veer, and voices clash,
One purpose binds, beneath freedom's sash.

This collection of poems was inspired by a central piece, a poem that served as the catalyst for this entire project. The recurring stanza, which begins with 'From freedom's spark to modern grace,' became the anchor that links each tribute to a U.S. President. This initial poem, crafted with the intention of capturing the essence of America's historical journey, birthed a unique connection throughout the entire collection.

The repeating stanza encapsulates the overarching themes of progress, resilience, and the indelible influence of presidential hands on the nation's destiny. It acts as a thread, seamlessly weaving together the stories of each president from George Washington to Joe Biden.

So, as you read through these verses, know that they all share a common heartbeat—a stanza that emerged from my initial exploration of freedom, trials, victories, and the shaping forces of presidential leadership. It serves as a poetic foundation, symbolizing the unity and continuity that bind the diverse narratives of the leaders who have guided the United States through its history.

From freedom's spark to modern grace,
Through trials met and victory's pace,
Each tale inscribed in history's rhyme,
Presidential hands that shaped our time.

From freedom's spark to modern grace,
They faced the dawn, each in their place,
Founders' vision, torch alight,
A nation forged, through day and night.

Through trials met and victory's pace,
From wars endured to rights embraced,
Leaders strode, with guiding hand,
United States, across the land.

Each tale inscribed in history's rhyme,
With triumphs etched and trials climb,
From humble roots to soaring might,
Each president, a guiding light.

Presidential hands that shaped our time,
From liberty's bell to modern's chime,
Though paths may veer, and voices clash,
One purpose binds, beneath freedom's sash.

This poem celebrates the historical journey of the United States, specifically focusing on the role of its presidents in shaping the nation. Let me break it down for you:

Structure and Style:

The poem consists of five quatrains, each with four lines. It follows an AABB rhyme scheme, where the first and second lines rhyme, and the third and fourth lines rhyme.

The language used is relatively formal and evokes a sense of patriotism and reverence.

Content:

First Stanza (Lines 1-4): The poem begins with a broad overview of the journey, starting from the inception of freedom ("freedom's spark") to the contemporary era ("modern grace"). It mentions the challenges faced and the victories achieved, emphasizing that each of these moments is recorded in the annals of history.

Second Stanza (Lines 5-8): This stanza elaborates on the early days of the nation, highlighting the commitment of individuals ("Founders") to the vision of building a nation. The metaphor of a torch alight symbolizes the enduring flame of their ideals in the creation of the United States.

Third Stanza (Lines 9-12): Here, the poem addresses the trials and triumphs faced by the nation. It acknowledges the sacrifices made in wars and the embracing of rights, all guided by leaders who played a crucial role in shaping the United States.

Fourth Stanza (Lines 13-16): This stanza underscores the idea that each tale of the nation is part of a larger historical narrative. The imagery of triumphs and trials, from humble beginnings to great power, reinforces the idea that the history of the United States is a dynamic and evolving story.

Fifth Stanza (Lines 17-20): The final stanza focuses on the role of the presidents in shaping the nation over time. It mentions specific symbols like "liberty's bell" and "modern's chime," representing the continuity and evolution of the American experience. Despite divergent paths and differing opinions, the poem emphasizes a common purpose rooted in freedom.

Overall Theme:

The overarching theme of the poem is the historical journey of the United States, with a specific emphasis on the role of its presidents in navigating challenges, leading the nation, and contributing to its development. The poem underscores a sense of unity and purpose beneath the banner of freedom.

In essence, the poem serves as a tribute to the nation's history, acknowledging the contributions of its leaders and the enduring spirit of freedom that binds the diverse experiences of the United States.

Joel Hawksley

Joel Hawksley is a co-founder of J & Washington and a US Army Veteran with over 20 years of executive-level management experience. Joel is a strategic thinker with a keen eye for analyzing economic conditions, identifying business trends, and anticipating market shifts.

Beyond his professional achievements, Joel has a deep passion for US history and a profound love for the English language, which he expresses through poetry. Graduate of the University of Central Florida, Nicholson School of Communication "Charge On."

www.ingramcontent.com/pod-product-compliance
Ingram Content Group UK Ltd.
Pitfield, Milton Keynes, MK11 3LW, UK
UKHW021646190726
13853UKWH00001B/91